Airbrushing for NAILS

Online Services

Delmar Online
To access a wide variety of Delmar products and services on the World Wide Web, point your browser to:
> **http://www.delmar.com**
> or email: info@delmar.com

thomson.com
To access International Thomson Publishing's home site for information on more than 34 publishers and 20,000 products, point your browser to:
> **http://www.thomson.com**
> or email: findit@kiosk.thomson.com

A service of I(T)P®

Milady SalonOvations

Airbrushing for NAILS

by
Elizabeth Anthony

Milady Publishing
(a division of Delmar Publishers)
3 Columbia Circle, P.O. Box 12519
Albany, New York 12212-2519

NOTICE TO THE READER

Publisher does not warrant or guarantee any of the products described herein or perform any independent analysis in connection with any of the product information contained herein. Publisher does not assume, and expressly disclaims, any obligation to obtain and include information other than that provided to it by the manufacturer.

The reader is expressly warned to consider and adopt all safety precautions that might be indicated by the activities herein and to avoid all potential hazards. By following the instructions contained herein, the reader willingly assumes all risks in connections with such instructions.

The publisher makes no representation or warranties of any kind, including but not limited to, the warranties of fitness for particular purpose or merchantability, nor are any such representations implied with respect to the material set forth herein, and the publisher takes no responsibility with respect to such material. The publisher shall not be liable for any special, consequential, or exemplary damages resulting, in whole or part, from the readers' use of, or reliance upon, this material.

Cover Design: Spiral Design Studio

Milady Staff
Publisher: Gordon Miller
Acquisitions Editor: Joseph Miranda
Project Editor: Annette Downs Danaher
Production Manager: Brian Yacur
Production and Art/Design Coordinator: Suzanne Nelson

COPYRIGHT © 1997
Milady Publishing
(a division of Delmar Publishers)
an International Thomson Publishing company

Printed in the United States of America
Printed and distributed simultaneously in Canada

For more information, contact:
Milady Publishing
3 Columbia Circle, Box 12519
Albany, New York 12212-2519

All rights reserved. No part of this work covered by the copyright hereon may be reproduced or used in any form or by any means—graphic, electronic, or mechanical, including photocopying, recording, taping, or information storage and retrieval systems—without the written permission of the publisher.

1 2 3 4 5 6 7 8 9 10   XXX   02 01 00 99 98 97

Library of Congress Cataloging-in-Publication Data

Anthony, Elizabeth
    Milady's airbrushing for nails / by Elizabeth Anthony.
        p.   cm.
    Includes index.
    ISBN: 1-56253-270-7
    1. Nail art (Manicuring)   1. Manicuring.   1. Airbrush art.
I. Milady Publishing Company.   I. Title.
TT958.3.A54   1996   96-11109
646.7'27–dc20   CIP

Contents

About the Author viii
Acknowledgments ix
Preface xii
Introduction xiv

PART 1: *Airbrushing Basics* 1

CHAPTER 1: The Airbrush 3
Types of Single-Action Airbrushes 5
    Types of Traditional Double-Action Airbrushes 7
    Types of New Technology Double-Action Airbrushes 12
    Maintenance and Cleaning Procedures for Single-Action and
    Traditional Double-Action Airbrushes 15
        Cleaning Supplies 16
        Step A: The Paint Color Change 16
        Step B: After the Service is Complete 18
        Step C: Periodic Maintenance 19
        Step D: End of the Day Cleaning 20
    Maintenance and Cleaning Procedures for New Technology Airbrushes 23
        Cleaning Supplies 24
        Step A: The Paint Color Change 24
        Step B: After the Service is Complete 24
        Step C: End of the Day Cleaning 25

CHAPTER 2: Air Sources and Hardware 26
Air Hoses 26
Air Sources 26
    Propellant Air Canister 27

Compressed Air Tank	28
Air Compressors	31
Air Pressure Regulators	35
Moisture Separator	36
Adapters	37
Manifolds	38

CHAPTER 3: Airbrush Paint and Supplies 40

Airbrush Nail Paint	41
Empty Paint Mixing Bottles	42
Aerosol Nail Paint	42
Airbrush Paint Cleaner	43
Airbrush Color Base Coat and Protective Coats	43
Base Coats on Natural Nails (Fingers and Toes!)	44
Base Coats on Artificial Nails (Sculptures, Wraps, etc.)	45
Design Tools	46
Practicing and Displaying Nail Tips	48

CHAPTER 4: Airbrush Nail Color Theory 50

Introduction to Nail Color Theory	50
Light is Everything to Color	50
The Color Wheel	51
Color Schemes	57
Mixing Paint Color	62
Paint Tints or Lightening Paint Color	63
Paint Shades or Darkening Paint Color	63
Dull Colors	64
Muted Colors	64
Pearl or Opalescent Colors	65
Color Matching	67
Paints to Fabric	67
Traditional Nail Polish	67
Cool and Warm Undertones	68
Color Placement on the Nails	69

CHAPTER 5: Getting Started and Finished 71

Set up and Practice	71
Working on Real People	74

CHAPTER 6: Troubleshooting Guide 77

CHAPTER 7: Introduction and Marketing of Airbrush Nail Services 86
    Introduction 86
    Airbrush Nail Services: The Give-Away! 88
    The Price List 89
    Business Building Strategies 91
        Custom-Blended Nail Color 91
    Conclusion 92
        Way to Market Your New Airbrushing Service......................... 92

PART 2: *Airbrushing Technicals* 95

  1. Solid Nail Color 97
  2. Nail Color Contour 99
  3. Two-color Fade (Color Blend) 101
  4. Multiple Color Fade 104
  5. Traditional French Manicure (With Optional Lunula) 107
  6. Chevron French Manicure (With Optional Chevron Lunula)........ 112
  7. Chevron French Manicure with Stripe 115
  8. Stencil Move Design 118
  9. Stencil Picture 121
10. Hand-cut Nail Masks—Striping 125
11. Pre-cut Nail Masks: Positive and Negative Use............................. 130
12. Pre-cut Mask Design with Stenciled Background 134
13. Stencil Pattern with Pre-cut Mask Design 138
14. Using a Stencil as a Design Template 141

Glossary 147
Index 153

About the Author

President, Progressive Nail Concepts, Inc.
Illinois Licensed Cosmetologist
Illinois Licensed Nail Technician
Illinois Licensed Nail Technology Instructor
Certified Esthetician & Makeup Artist

Elizabeth Anthony started out as a nail salon employee, and eventually became a full-service salon owner. She was a professional nail school owner, a distributor of professional nail products, and a designer of two professional nail product systems. With more than 17 years of experience, she is an accomplished educator, competition judge, motivational speaker and consultant to the beauty industry.

Elizabeth lectures and teaches seminars around the world for professional nail technicians, industry educators, cosmetologists and other salon specialists. She teaches all forms of nail technology, specializing in Sanitation & Disinfection, Nail Disorders & Diseases, Chemistry of Artificial Nail Products, Successful Salon Marketing and Business, and Airbrushed Nail Color & Nail Art. She has written articles for and been quoted by *Beauty Store Business, Nailpro Magazine, Nails Magazine, Airbrush Magazine, Modern Salon Magazine,* and *Glamour*. And, she has a column on airbrushing nails in each issue of *Airbrush Magazine*. Elizabeth Anthony Institute, a division of Progressive Nail Concepts, Inc., is recognized by the State of Illinois as a Continuing Education Sponsor.

Acknowledgments

Lord, thank you for this opportunity to share my knowledge and experience with the professional nail industry. I have been blessed with many friends, associates and mentors.

I want to thank Bruce Brunsfeld for being a positive force in my life and helping me accomplish my dreams. He has shared this journey offering his love, patience, and encouragement every step of the way. I thank the Lord for bringing our lives together.

I want to thank my son Stephen for his love and acceptance. It has not been an easy time living with a single, working mom! We have shared many nights of "homework" together—his schoolwork and my book. Over the years he has been my motivation and inspiration.

I want to thank my mother, Nellie Baker, who has been my rock of Gibraltar. I never thought I was as strong as my mother, but over the years I have learned that I have inherited her tenacity. There have been many ups and downs, but I could always count on her love and support. Thank you, Mom! I could not have done it without you.

I want to thank my father, Ernie Baker, and his wife, Carol Baker, for being there whenever I needed them. I learned important business and life lessons from my father. My father shared his personal secrets of success with me—honorable business ethics and being the best you can be at your profession! I am very fortunate to have had such supportive and loving parents.

I want to thank my sister, Jeanette Grondin, and her husband, Michael Grondin, for being there whenever I needed them. Thank you for being my sounding board and helping to preserve my sanity. Your loving friendship is a precious gift!

I want to thank Sandi Nidetz for her friendship, loyalty, creativity, and thoughtful direction throughout the years and during this project. Sandi has been my right-arm for many years, teaching seminars and helping me with whatever needed to be done. Sandi airbrushed the nail tips and artwork in the color theory chapter of this book. Thank you for running the office so I could complete this book. Thank you for your wisdom and humor when the going got rough. Thank you for everything!

I want to thank Lisa Kathan for her friendship and support throughout the years. Her personal experience, enthusiasm and professional feedback have been invaluable. Lisa tested my skills as a teacher many years ago and built my self-confidence. Since then, she has been teaching my airbrush seminars and is living proof that if you want to be successful, you will be successful! Thank you for all your help and encouragement!

I want to thank Deneen Daniels and all the new airbrush nail educators I have had the honor to work with. You are the future of professional airbrush nail color!

I want to thank Shirley Younger for showing me the meaning of true friendship. You were always there to help, offer a "pep" talk, or just listen. You define the word special. We need to "do lunch"!

I want to thank the thousands of students that I have had the privilege to work with. I have learned so much from everyone. This project would not have been possible without the years of experience I have had teaching airbrushed nail color.

I want to thank the airbrush manufacturers and their associates who have given me many opportunities to grow over the years. Through their referrals and consulting work I have grown in the airbrush and beauty industry.

I have had the honor and great fortune to observe and learn from the best airbrush artists in the professional airbrush industry. There are many people that I would like to thank, and you know who you are. Without your selfless sharing at tradeshows, workshops and phone conversations the airbrush industry would not be where it is today! There are a few special people I must mention.

I want to thank Dennis Hoey, formerly of Starmist Cosmetics, for introducing me to the world of airbrush makeup and nail art. He was a generous teacher and skilled at sharing his knowledge. Over the years he introduced me to products and individuals that expanded my horizons.

I want to thank Robert Sanders, formerly of Colormist Products and Nails By Design, for introducing me to the possibilities of airbrushed nail color in the salon. His programs were ahead of that time (mid to late 1980's). He most influenced my style of airbrushing nails. His methods of teaching airbrush nail color gave me the foundation that my current program of education evolved from. It was tough when he decided to leave the beauty industry, but his departure forced me to expand my knowledge in the field of airbrushing nails.

I want to thank Dru Blair for his insight, encouragement and admiration. It might have been difficult entering into "the boy's club" of professional airbrush artists if you hadn't been so kind to introduce me to everyone. Our "TV Spot" in Atlanta is a moment in history!

I would like to thank Mickey and Laura Harris for inviting me to be a part of the Board of Advisors for The American Association of Airbrush Artists. Thank you for permitting me to share airbrush nail concepts with the readers of AIRBRUSH

MAGAZINE. Thank you, Mickey, for taking the time to help me with some big decisions.

I want to thank Tim Mitchell and Robert Paschall for sharing their experiences and optimism for the airbrush nail industry. Your assistance and personal successes have been constant inspiration.

I had hoped to give Ted Eckaus my book personally. Unfortunately, he left this world too soon. Ted was the first person who helped me airbrush nails. I bought an airbrush and when I called for help, he was there. Ted was always available to offer advice, encouragement and counsel. Ted encouraged me to share my personal experience at tradeshows for his company and to start teaching airbrushed nails. When he felt that he couldn't answer a question, he never hesitated to connect me with someone who could help. That is how I originally connected with Dennis Hoey, my first formal airbrush teacher. I know that I am not alone in saying that Ted Eckaus was there for many of us and he is desperately missed. I take comfort knowing that Ted is still with us in spirit and in our hearts. Thank you, Ted. We miss you.

The publisher would like to thank the following professionals for their time and expertise in reviewing this manuscript: Debbie Mack, Chicago, IL; Constance Smith, St. Louis, MO; Patti Rossi, Bricktown, NJ; and Barbara Bealer, Bethlehem, PA.

There are many more people for one reason or another that shall remain nameless. You know who you are. There are so many who have given so much. Thank you and God bless!

Preface

People outside the professional nail industry often wonder how those of us in it would want to do nails for a living.

Well, after eighteen years, I am still "doing nails" and thrilled about it!

I consider myself lucky that I am able to teach a profession that I love so much. The nail profession has become a fascinating and financially rewarding career for those who have chosen it.

I learned about airbrushing fingernails in a trade magazine many years ago. I would faithfully attend the trade shows, looking for this technique, hoping to get a glimpse of how it looked and how it was done. Unfortunately, since I was located in the heart of the "conservative" midwest, none of the companies that were promoting "airbrushed nails" ventured into my area. So I went to the local craft store and asked if they had airbrushes that would work on fingernails. The store manager did not know a lot about airbrushing, but he showed me an airbrush that he thought might work for me. I invested in the airbrush, hose, compressor and some paint and with help from one of my nail technicians we began the journey into the unknown world of airbrushing fingernails.

From the start, I was having all types of problems trying to operate the airbrush and maintain it. Fortunately the manufacturer was close to my salon in Illinois. I called the company and was introduced to a man who would always be there to help me. His name was Ted Eckaus, and he was very patient in explaining how to properly operate and clean the airbrush. He was honest and told me he knew very little about how to spray on nails but referred me to some people that he hoped could help. After I had mastered the art of airbrushing fingernails, Ted Eckaus referred all nail technicians to me.

I began to travel to different seminars to see what I could learn. Most were offered on the West or East coasts. I was fortunate to take seminars with Mr. Dennis Hoey, who specialized in airbrush makeup, and Mr. Robert Sanders, a talented graphic artist who had started decorating fingernails. I attended many seminars on airbrushing but learned the most from these two talented men. You can learn many things from books and videos, but nothing replaces hands-on training with a qualified instructor.

Airbrushing and nail art were bringing quite a bit of attention to my little salon in the northwest suburbs of Chicago. My nail technicians had the option to learn airbrushing. Most chose to learn once they saw the incredible income potential, which we will talk more about later. Other nail technicians in the area had heard of airbrushing but could find no one to help them learn it. I began offering formal training programs which developed quickly into a full-time professional nail school that I owned for three years.

The demands for me to take my educational programs on the road became irresistible, so I began to travel to different locations nationwide. I became a national consultant and educator for all forms of nail technology. Teaching airbrushing has kept me the busiest. The manufacturers kept referring me to professional beauty distributors and schools since they knew my program would support the use of their airbrushes.

The success of my program may be attributed to the fact that I have been a nail technician, salon owner, professional nail product distributor and school owner. I know what works from my own experiences. This has given my curriculum an edge over so many others. These were artists who had airbrushed in other fields and saw the nail as another canvas. They may be able to teach airbrushing, but they couldn't teach the nail technician ways to introduce and make money airbrushing in the salon environment.

Due to the increased interest in airbrushing nails, the need for a textbook has evolved. I have designed this book using the standards of my training program. For the new student this book may be used as a guide to choose equipment and to assist them in using that equipment profitably. I hope this book will serve as a reference for the maintenance of airbrush equipment, that it will help technicians increase their income with airbrushing techniques, and provide some new methods to achieve different designs. I am happy to be able to offer my methods of airbrushing nails in textbook form. The information that was not available when I was starting out is now available for you—to help you to avoid learning the "hard way!"

Introduction

Airbrushing nails has been by far the most profitable nail service I ever introduced to my clientele. When I first started airbrushing nails, my salon already offered an extensive array of handpainted and jeweled nail art; airbrushing was an extension of our selection. The airbrushed nail designs had a unique satin finish, a sophisticated appearance and dried very quickly. Airbrushed nail art promptly became the favored art form for nail decorating in our salon.

These remarkable results made me evaluate the airbrushing service closer. The airbrushed nail dried within ten to fifteen minutes, which was quite revolutionary over ten years ago. The airbrushed coating was much thinner than traditional nail polish and had a smooth appearance. The airbrushed nail color had no brush strokes, even in pearlescent or frosted nail color, or unevenness of pigment which is common with traditional nail polish. With these benefits in mind, I started to use the airbrush to apply solid nail color for every one of my clients. They were thrilled with the results. Their nails appeared thinner (a traditional nail polish coating is much bulkier than an airbrushed nail color) and many felt that the airbrushed nail color lasted better than the traditional nail polish. My clients were impressed with how superior the nail color finish looked and felt.

French manicures were very popular with our clients. These manicures were neutral, so the client did not have to worry about what they were going to wear the next week. With an airbrush, the French manicure took half the time to apply and was perfect every time. There was no bump, unevenness or thickness on the nail tip color. The airbrushed French manicure dried within minutes unlike those applied with traditional nail polish that required four to eight hours. When the French manicure was airbrushed it took less time to add special effects such as a moon or lunula, to the cuticle area for a very natural look.

In addition to the French manicures, I started experimenting with multiple color applications called color fades or color blends. For the color fade, the nail technician may start with a soft pink near the cuticle, a deep pink through the body of the nail and then sprays a rich red at the free edge. The three colors softly fade into each other, creating a very subtle but elegant choice for a conservative client.

Subtle color blends added a bit of excitement to a previous monotonous color, but not enough that they couldn't wear it to the office. Before airbrushed nail color, the client was limited to a change between a few of her favorite colors each week—now she could wear all three at the same time.

As clients came to prefer airbrushed nail color to traditional nail polish, I began to notice a change in my income—it was rising. After careful evaluation of my books, I realized why I was experiencing this increase. When I began airbrushing nails, I also started charging a small additional amount for the service, say three to eight dollars. But I was accomplishing the airbrushed nail color in the same amount of time that it previously took to polish their nails. In other words, I was generating three to eight dollars extra per client each day without adding any time to my schedule. Do a little multiplication and you will see that adds up to $24 to $56 more a day without working any longer. Airbrushing nails, every nail that came through my door—not just nail art—was the secret to my success in airbrushing. In the marketing chapter, I will outline my methods of introducing airbrush nail color and nail art to your clients.

The first step to becoming a successful airbrush nail artist is to pick the equipment that works best for you. In the next chapter, we will carefully review the types of airbrush equipment and products available on the market. This chapter will help you choose the equipment that best suits your needs. If you already have some airbrush equipment, it will help you use your equipment properly and evaluate its effectiveness against what else is available. Just as you have your favorite tools to accomplish a set of nails or manicure, you will find different people prefer different things when they airbrush nails, too. Most importantly, you want to be able to accomplish your best work in the least amount of time. But remember, airbrushing nails takes lots of practice to master, just like sculpturing nails! Remember your first set and how long it took to finish? Remember the weeks of practice to get it just right? The same rule applies to airbrushed nails. It takes practice to get it right. Many times people blame the "problems" or difficulties on the equipment. When you know what to expect from your equipment, it will be easier to evaluate the equipment and your results.

After you have chosen your equipment, you will move to some basic exercises to familiarize yourself with the airbrush. You will start on paper and then move to practice nail tips. You do not require live models to practice airbrushing. When you are comfortable with your results on nail tips, you may start practicing on friends, family and co-workers. When you move to "real" people, you will have to learn how to hold their hand comfortably but effectively. You will also master the skill of "cleanup." When airbrushing nails, there is an overspray of paint onto the cuticle area of the finger or toe. This area needs to be cleaned after the paint has been sealed and protected. We will discuss these techniques when you start airbrushing on nail tips in later chapters. The technical chapters are placed in sequential order. I recommend learning your color theory, then doing each technique in the order it appears in the book. Each technical builds on the skills mastered in the previous exercise. Each correctly completed nail tip will build a collection that you may display to introduce the concept of airbrushed nail color and nail art to your clients. After you complete the lessons in this book, your clients will have a choice of nail color and nail art unlike anything you have offered before.

Most of you opened this book to learn how to airbrush nail art. This book will teach you how to produce incredible nail art. Along the way, I hope to share more than just airbrushed nail art with you. I know that most every one would like to make more money. If you fall into that category, please be sure to read this book carefully and use the proven methods outlined for increasing your income with airbrushed nail color and nail art. After you have given these methods a try, let me know how you are doing!